DOODLE AND DRAW
EVERYTHING

PaRragon.

Add bunny passengers to the train.

DOODLE
AND DRAW
EVERYTHING

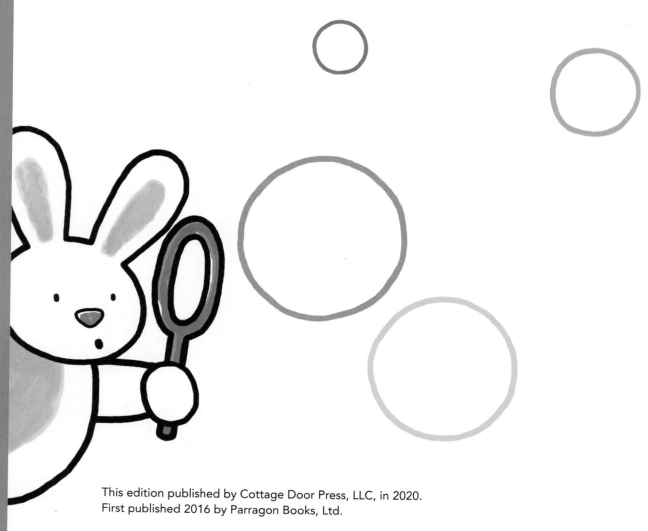

This edition published by Cottage Door Press, LLC, in 2020.
First published 2016 by Parragon Books, Ltd.

Copyright © 2020 Cottage Door Press, LLC
5005 Newport Drive, Rolling Meadows, Illinois 60008

Written by Susan Fairbrother
Illustrated by Bella Bee and Mike Garton

ISBN: 978-1-64638-012-1

Printed in China

Parragon Books is an imprint of Cottage Door Press, LLC.
Parragon Books® and the Parragon® logo are registered trademarks of Cottage Door Press, LLC.

Doodle something for Mouse to pull.

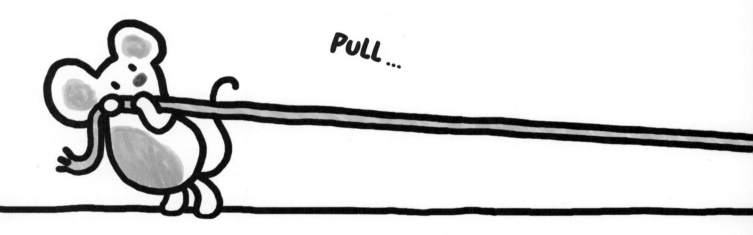

PULL ...

Doodle something for Mouse to push.

PUSH ...

Happy

sad

Triangles could be ...

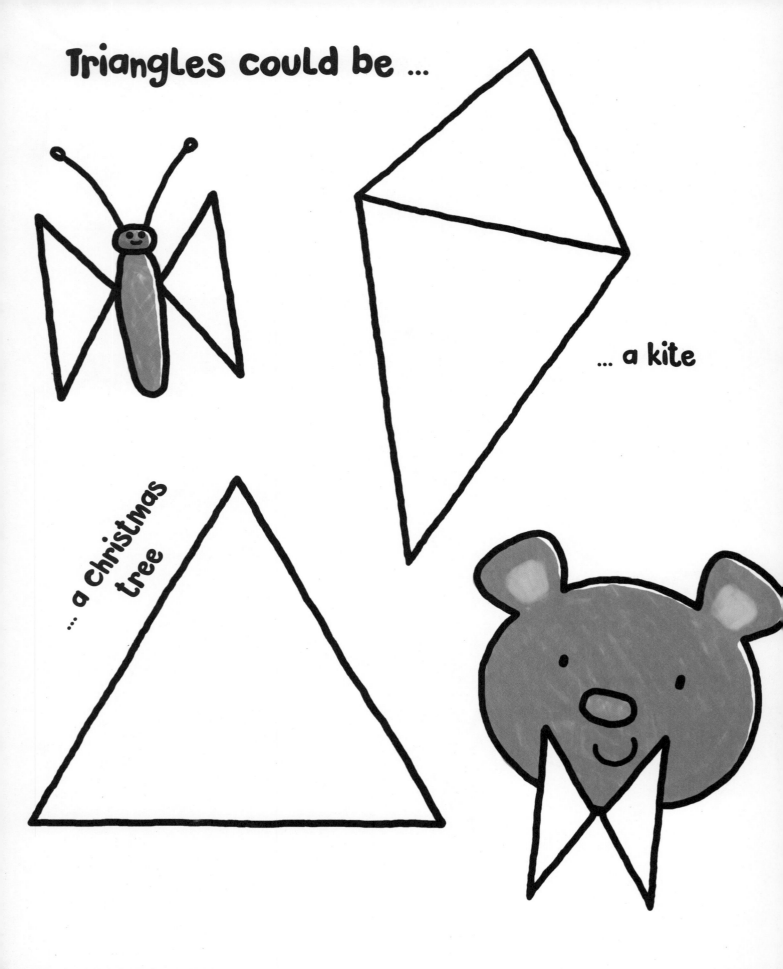

... a kite

... a christmas tree

Triangles have three sides.
Draw more triangle pictures.

Add 3 flags to the palace.

A fairy tale needs a prince
and a princess. Add them here.

scary!
Add more spiders
with 8 Legs.

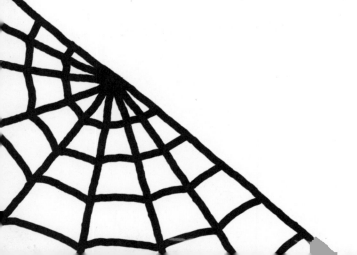

Doodle more LONG snakes and more SHORT snakes.

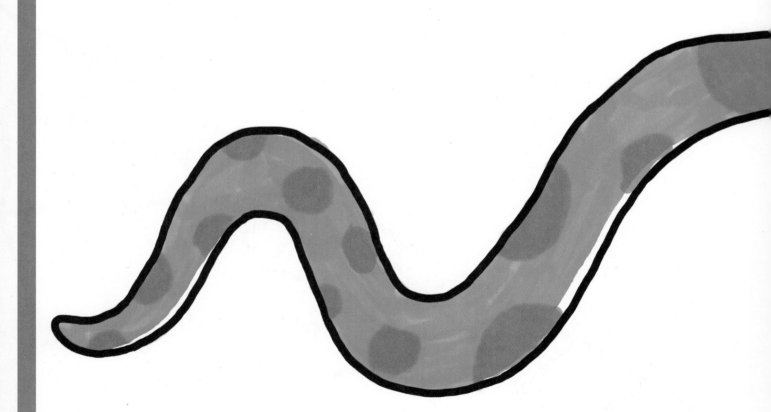

Draw more animals climbing up the hill and some zipping DOWN.

FULL

EMPTY

Fill up the empty milkshake glasses!

Add more birds ABOVE the water.

Doodle more
fish **BELOW**
the waves.

The treasure map has been LOST.
Doodle a new one.

The treasure has been FOUND! Add more coins to the chest.

squares could be ...

... a present

... a robot

squares have 4 sides.
Draw more square pictures!

Add 3 more apples to the tree.

Doodle 2 more butterfly friends.

Moo!

Draw 1 more cow on the hill.

This show is very funny! Draw 4 clowns on the stage.

Haha!

Triangle spikes!

Add triangles to every dinosaur to make them all really spiky.

RAINY

Give each bear a
colorful umbrella.

SUNNY

Give all the cats sunglasses.

Draw yourself in the mirror.

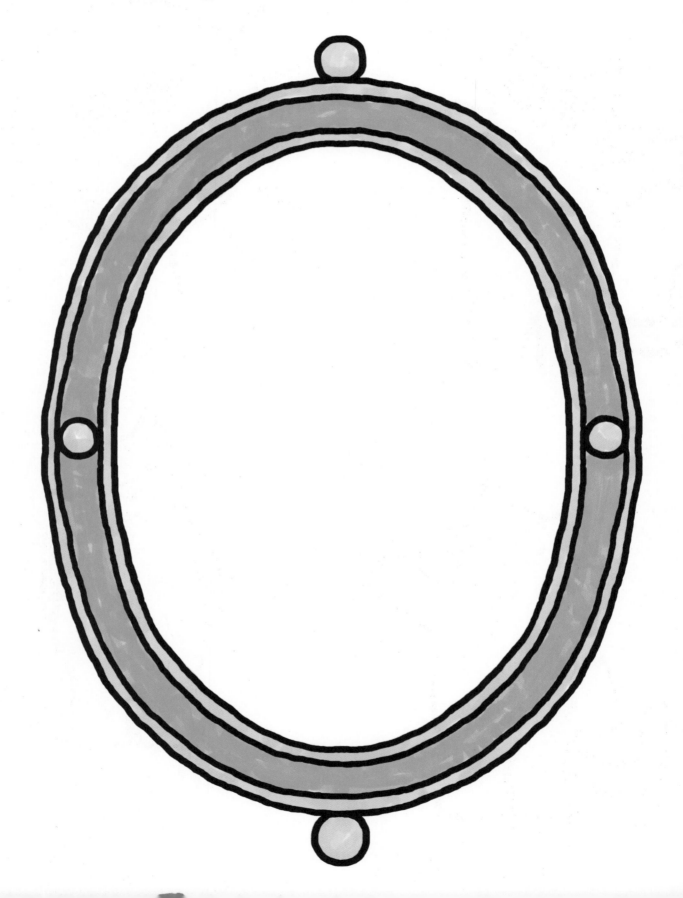

Doodle your family in the frames!

Add 3 more cookies to the plate.

Doodle 4 more pieces of fruit.

Draw 2 more chocolate chip cookies.

Add 5 more cupcakes.

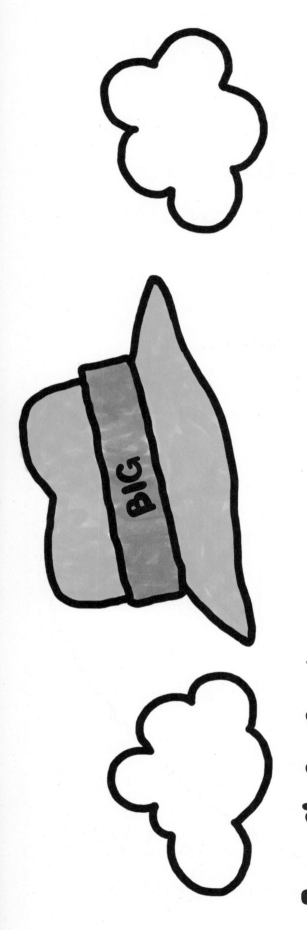

Fee, fi, fo, fum!
Draw the rest
of the giant.

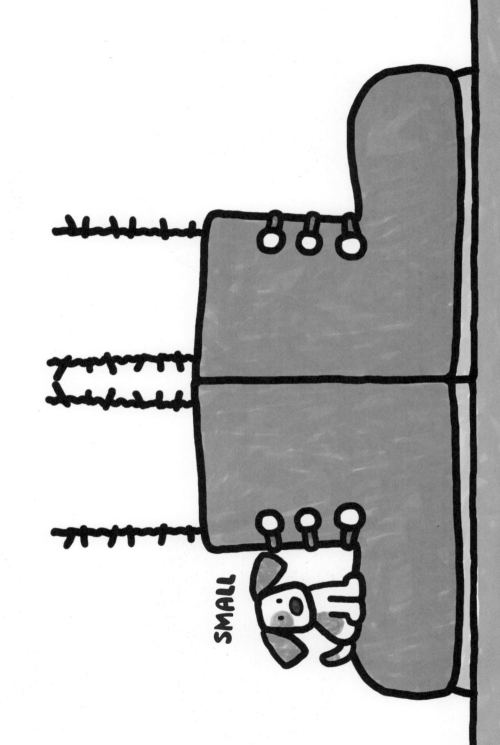

Give everyone a new hat!

Bears love picnics!

CIRCLES
Add more apples.

TRIANGLES
Add more pizza slices.

Draw more stars in the sky and owls on the branch.

NIGHT

DAY

Doodle more clouds and little rabbits!

Who lives in the castle?

where is the captain?

Ready to race? Doodle more cars on the track.

DOWN

Have you seen my friends?
Doodle lots more penguins on the ice.

Draw a house for the mouse.

Draw a hat for the cat.

HaLf pictures! Doodle the other side.

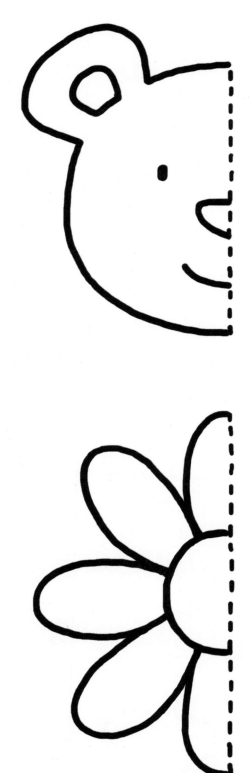

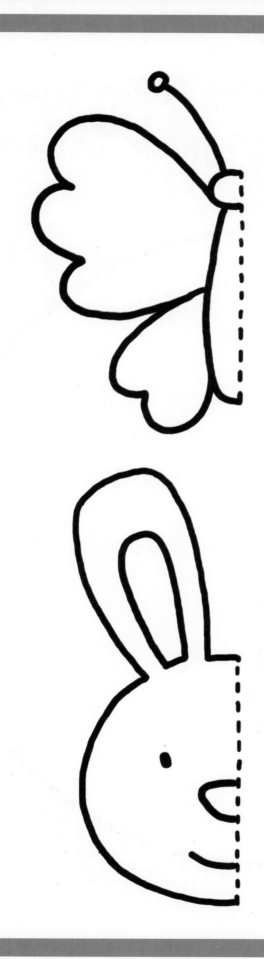

What's cooking? Doodle 3 sausages in the pan.

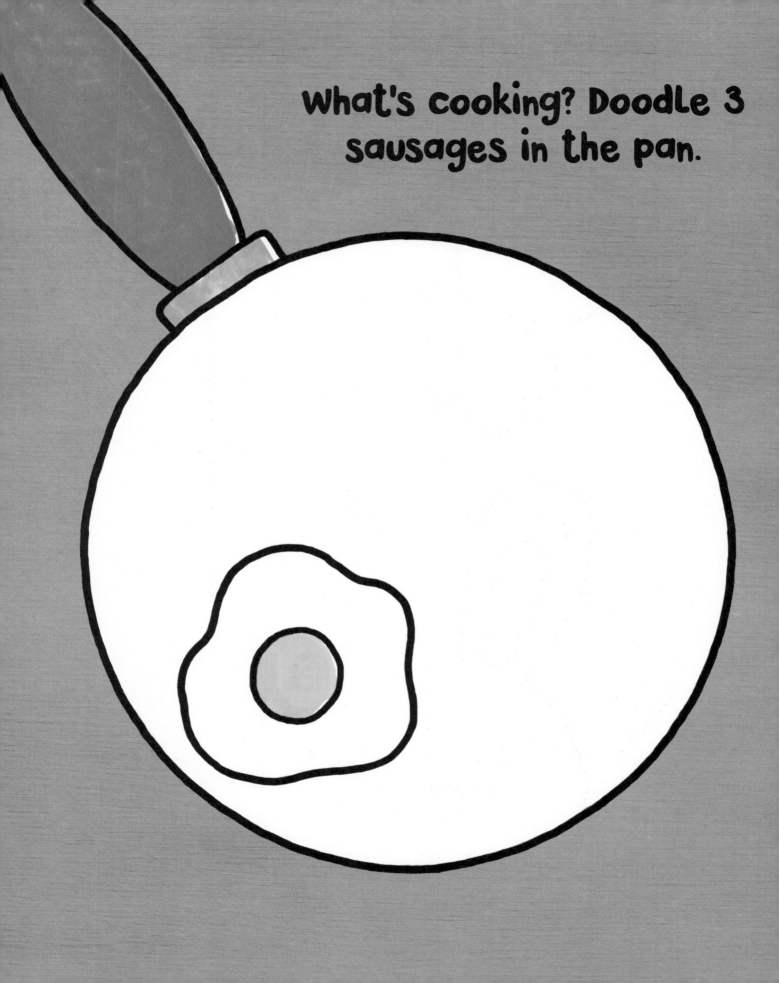

Fill the page with circle bubbles!

Complete the city.
Draw TALL skyscrapers and SHORT houses.

Doodle lots of tasty popcorn.
Who's got the most?

Rabbit

Mouse

Bird

Wow, what a sight! Add purple fireworks.

Add green fireworks here.

Give each monkey a pair of boots and a big puddle to splash in!

Doodle an alien friend peeking out from each crater!

Add a red balloon to every string.

Draw a fish on the end of each Line.

Give everyone a pair of silly glasses!

Draw 2 more colorful kites.

Draw BIG socks and BIG underpants on the clotheslines.

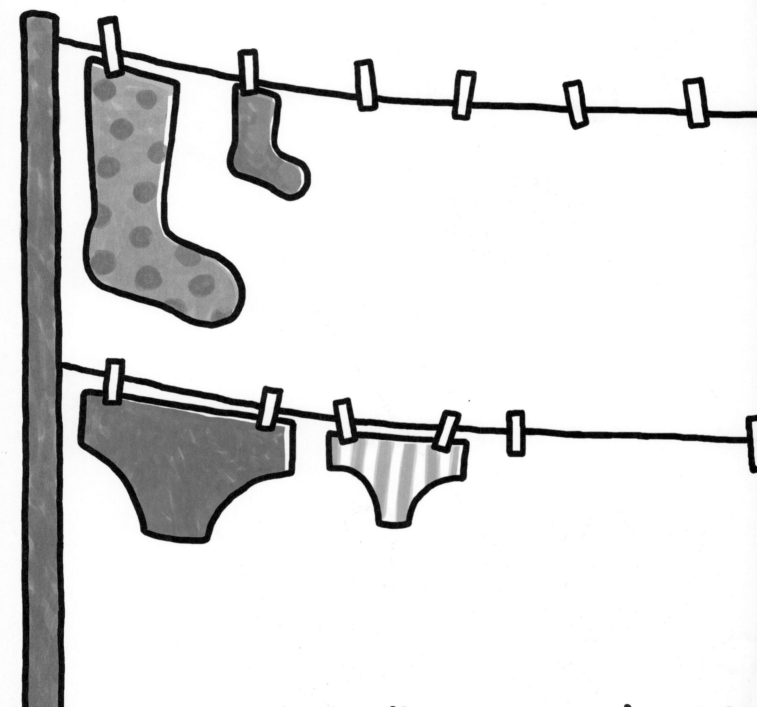

Doodle SMALL socks and SMALL underpants, too!

Draw some zigzag lines.

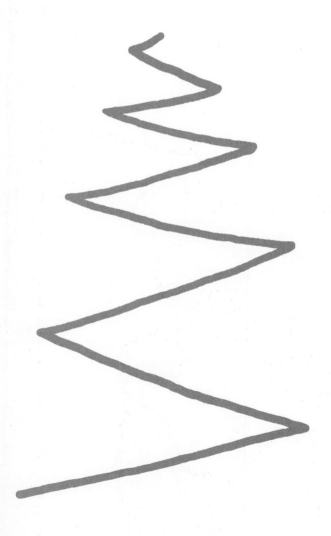

Draw a zigzag road down the mountain.

SPRING

Draw Lots of Leaves on the tree.

FALL

Add fallen leaves
in a big pile!

Draw 5 more footprints on each trail.

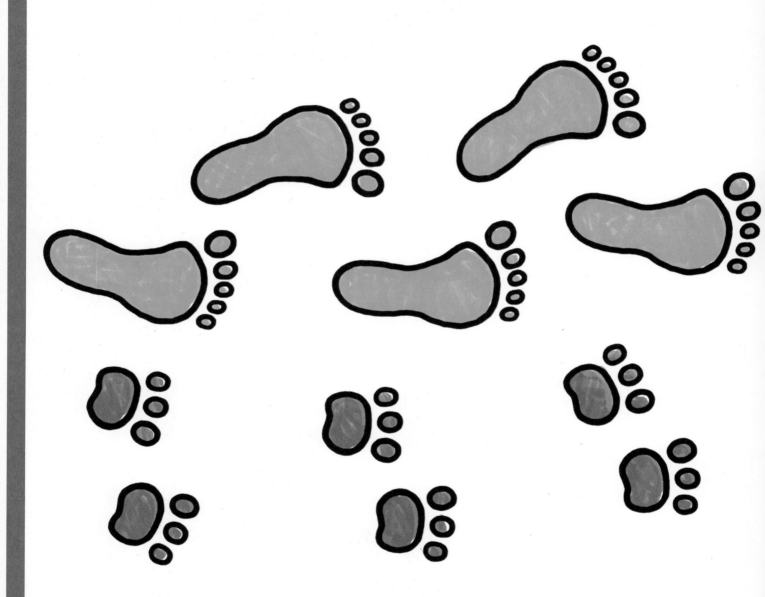

Doodle 2 rabbits in each burrow.

Draw a wig for the pig.

Draw a dog on the log.

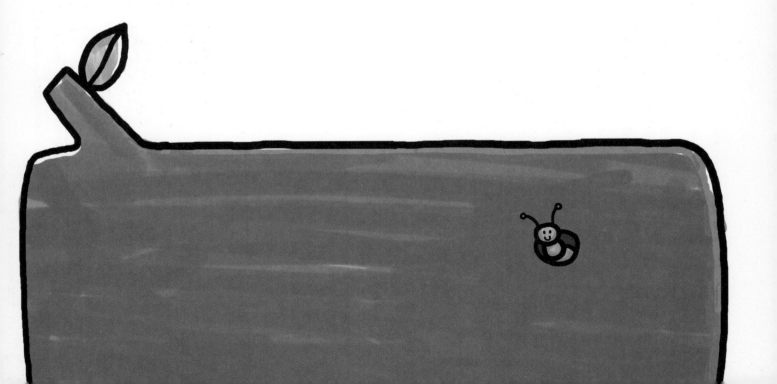

Draw some more feathery friends!

How many birds
did you doodle?

Complete the pizzas with more triangle slices.

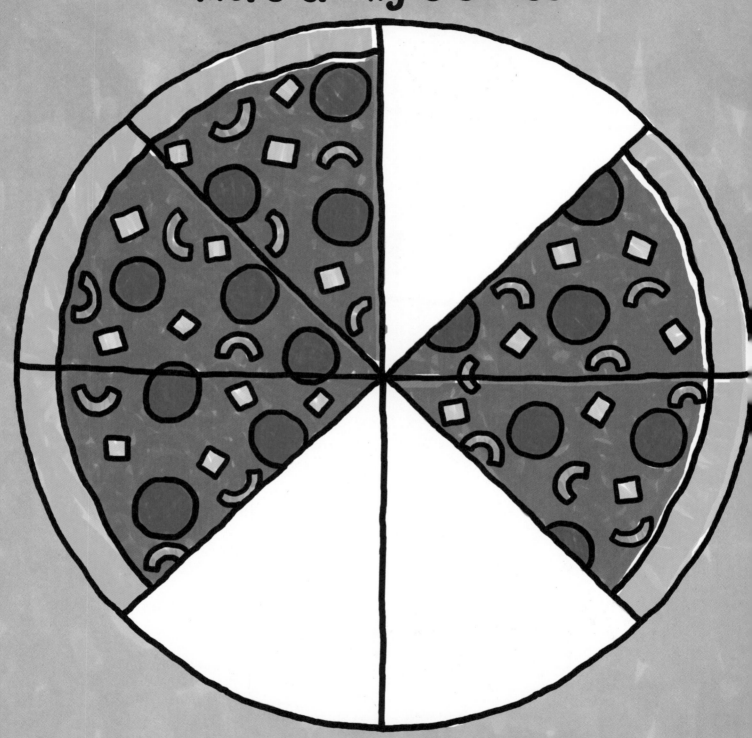

Who's on the seesaw?

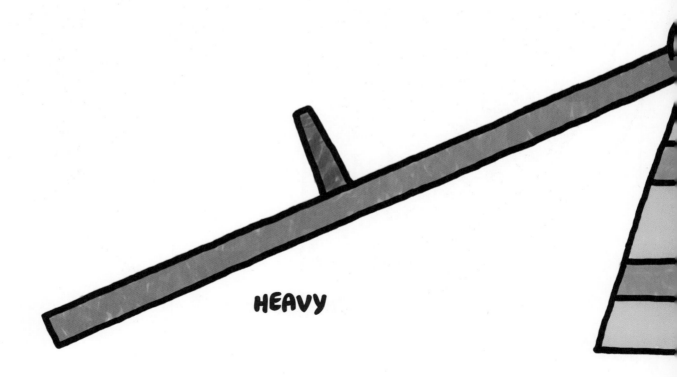

HEAVY

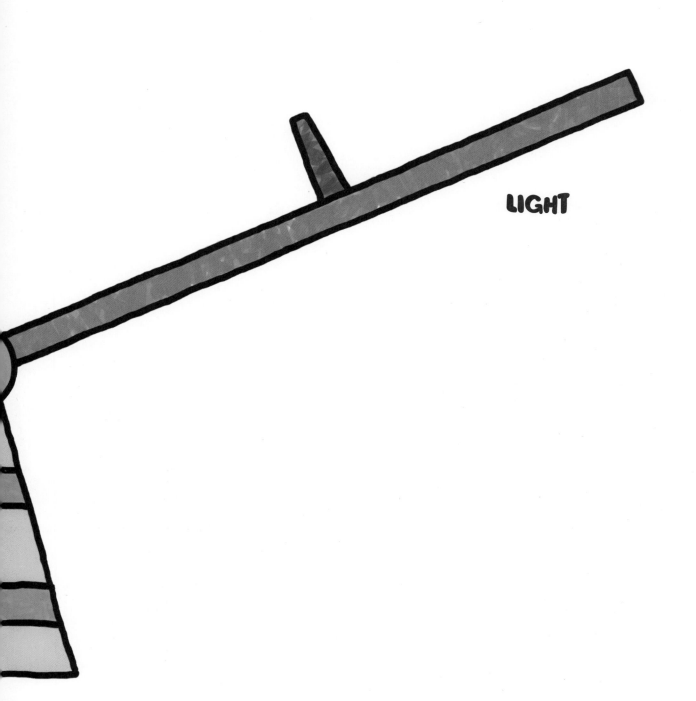

LIGHT

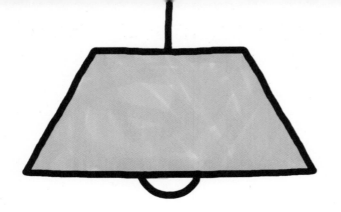

DRAW SOMEONE INSIDE.

DRAW SOMEONE OUTSIDE.

Doodle the missing shoes to make 4 pairs.

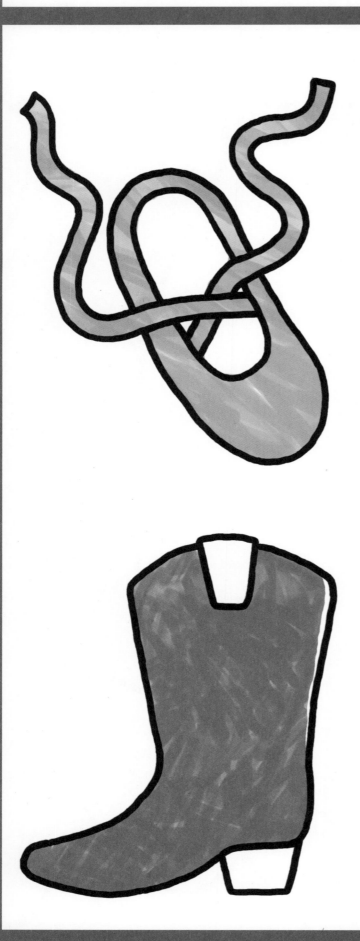

Doodle more cats up at the top.

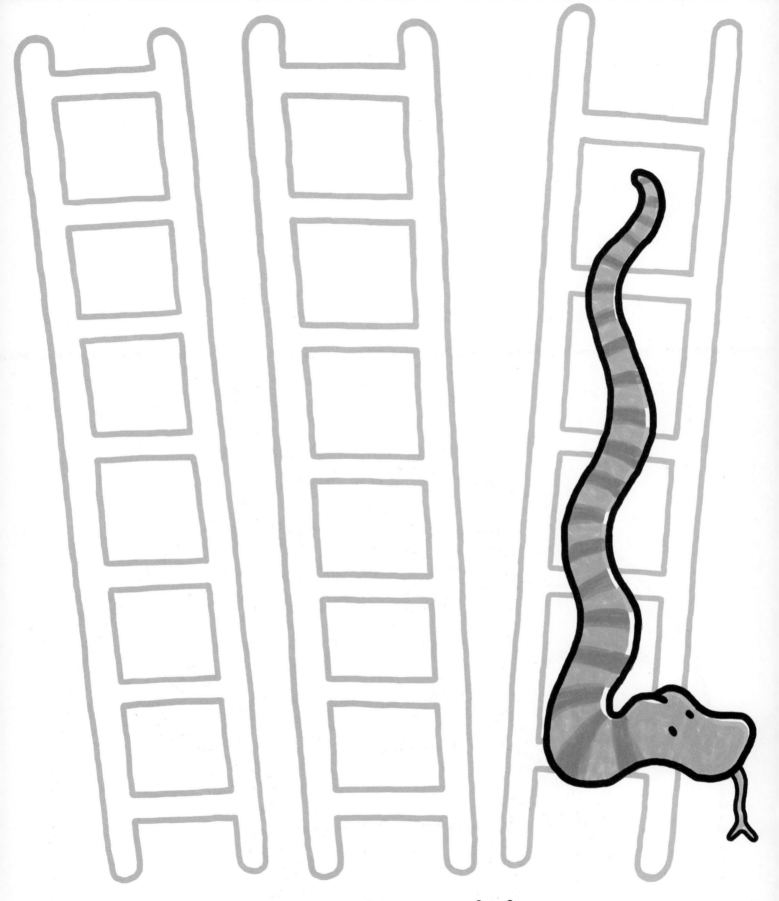

Draw more snakes sliding DOWN.

Who's going OVER this bridge?

CLip, clop, clip, clop!

Who's UNDER this bridge?

Doodle **LONG** tails
for the **monkeys.**

Hedgehog has SHORT spikes. Add Lots more.

Sad Snowman! Doodle him a friend.

Happy Snowman! Draw another.

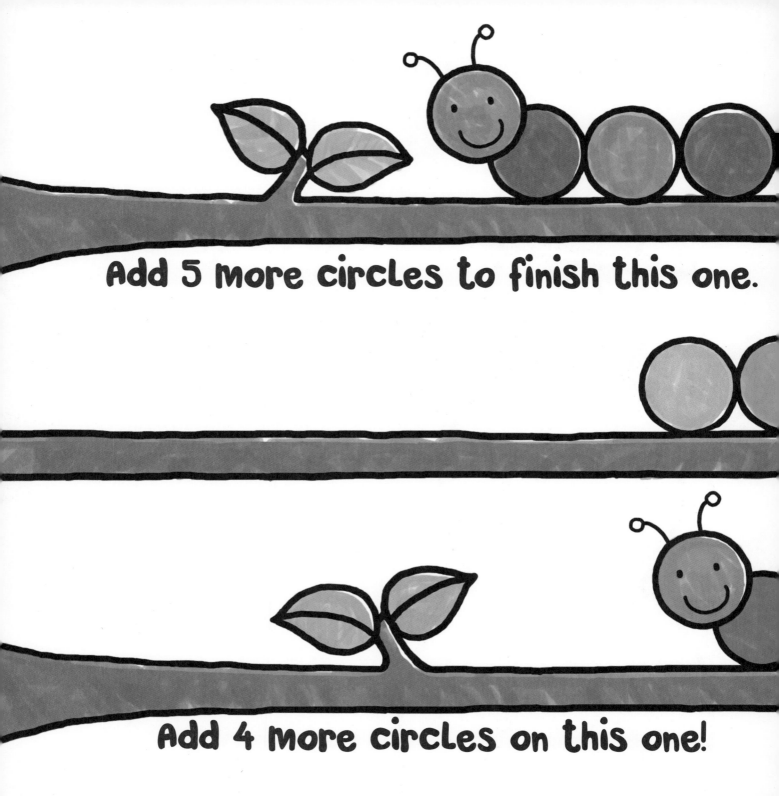

Add 5 more circles to finish this one.

Add 4 more circles on this one!

Add 4 circles to finish this caterpillar.

Add 3 more circles on this one!

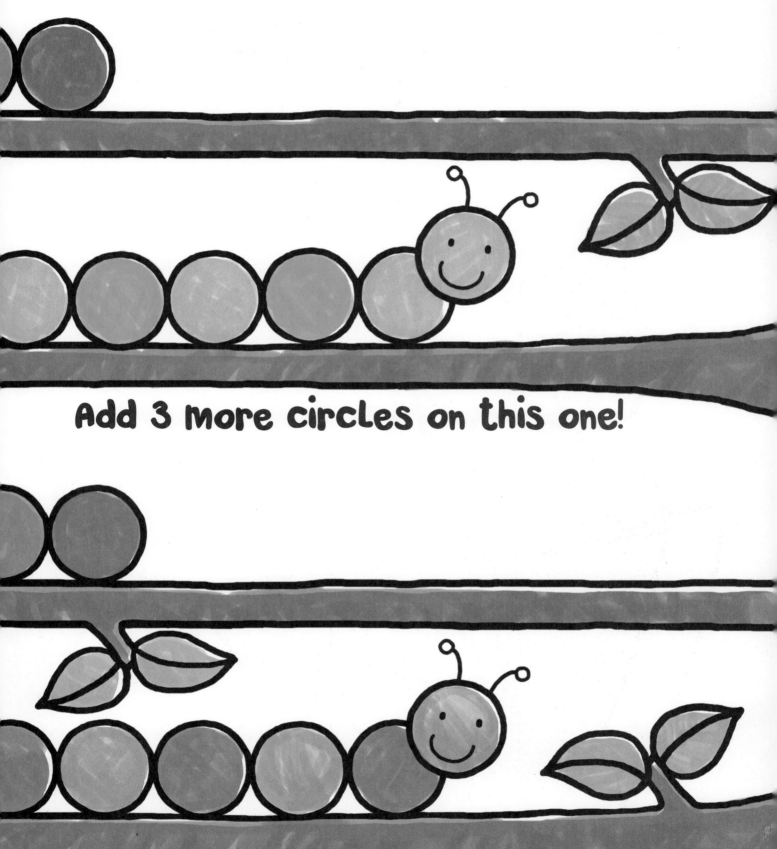

Add a big sail to the ship.

Draw a pirate in each porthole.

Doodle more water to make the plants grow!

They've grown! Doodle pretty flowers.

Doodle a door!

CLOSED

Who's at the door?

OPEN

Circles could be...

... a ball

... a pizza

Circles have no corners.
Draw more circle pictures!

Draw 3 more passengers on the ferris wheel.

Doodle some sea creatures!

Draw 2 more crabs.

Doodle an
owl wide
AWAKE.

Doodle a
mouse fast
ASLEEP.

Doodle lots of different houses.

This house
needs windows!

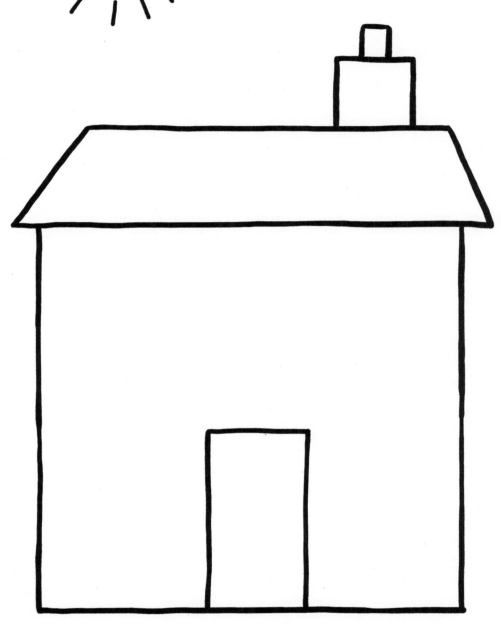

Finish the line patterns.

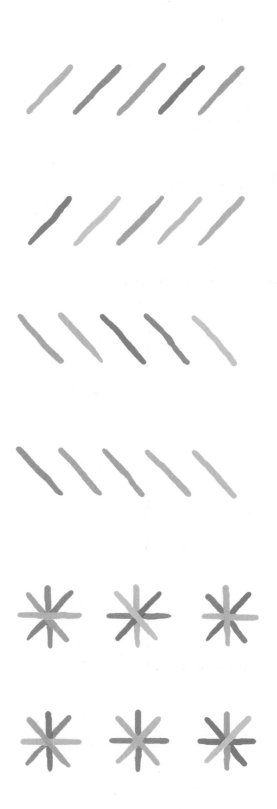

Use your patterns to draw rain and snow.

The spider
needs a web!
Finish the
Lines.

Trace some web patterns, then add spiders.

Try drawing some swirls.

Add swirls
to the woolly
coats of the sheep.

Baa baa

Use the dots as a guide to color in each sea creature.

Doodle a cloud pattern.

Draw a star pattern in the night sky.

Trace the lines to make a spiky, zigzag pattern!

Trace the lines to make a curly, swirly pattern!

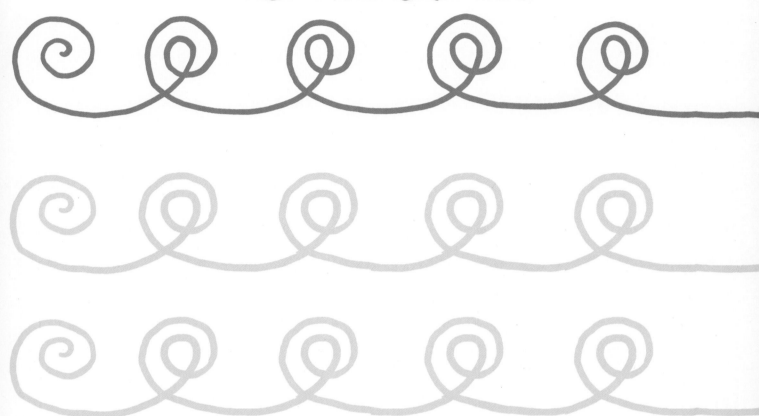

Finish the brick pattern with rectangles.

Caterpillar counting!

count 4 caterpillar babies
and finish their patterns.

Add more circle patterns.

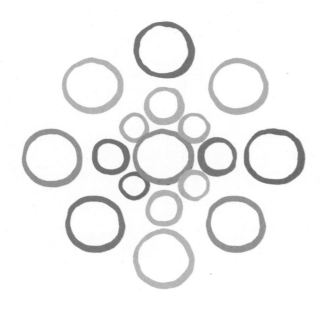

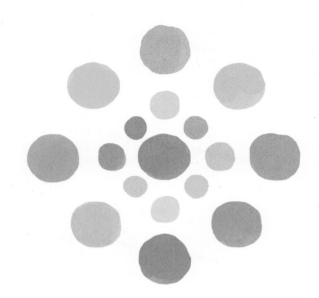

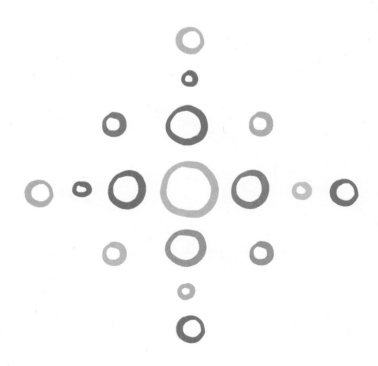

Complete the rainbow patterns!

Gloves and mittens.
Make some woolly patterns!

finish the shell patterns.

10 silly snakes... give them all stripes!

Try a swirl.

Try a fan.

Doodle more squares and rectangles.

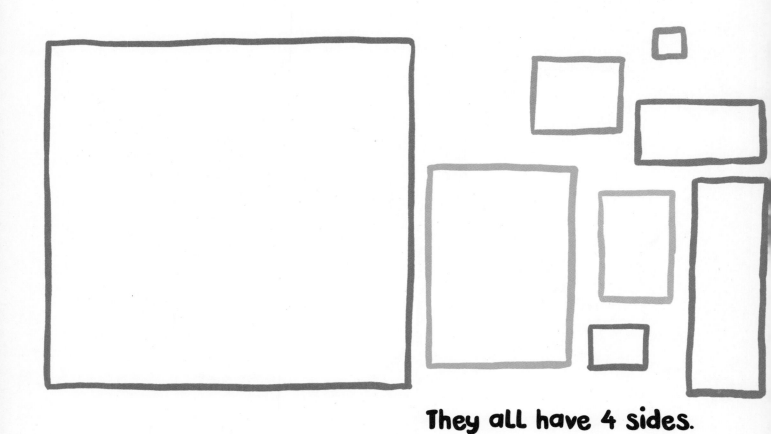

They all have 4 sides.

Add a pattern of squares to this robot.

cupcakes, yum!

Add swirl and sprinkle patterns.

Finish the zigzag patterns.

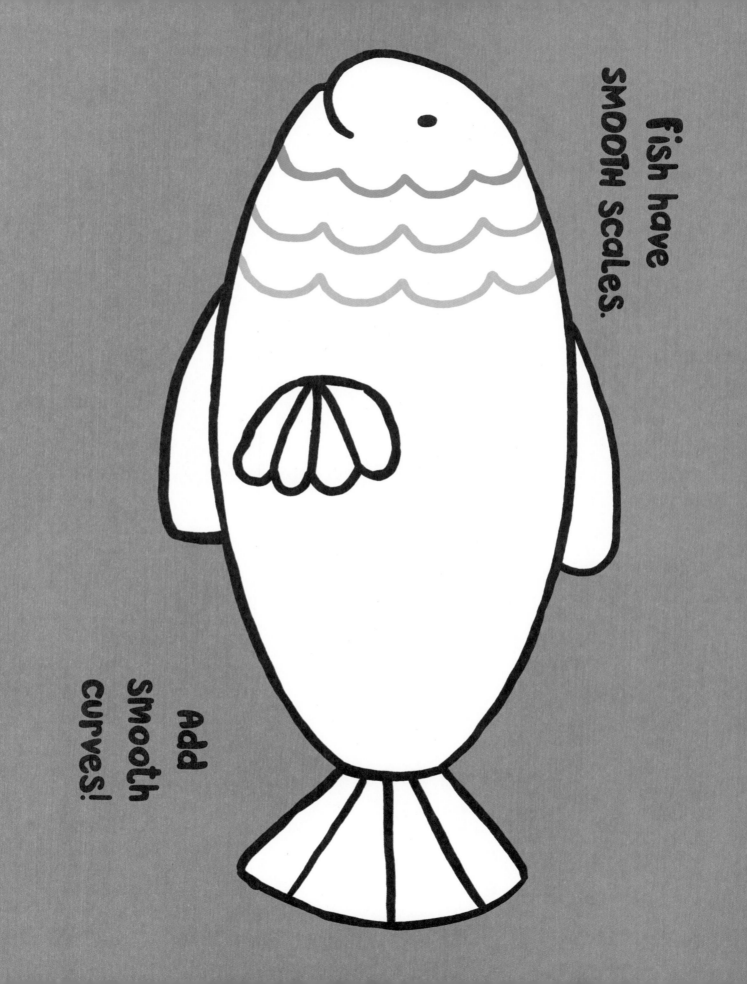

fish have
SMOOTH scales.

Add
smooth
curves!

Crocodiles have
spiky scales.
Add zigzags!

Finish each sun with circles or triangles to make them all shine!

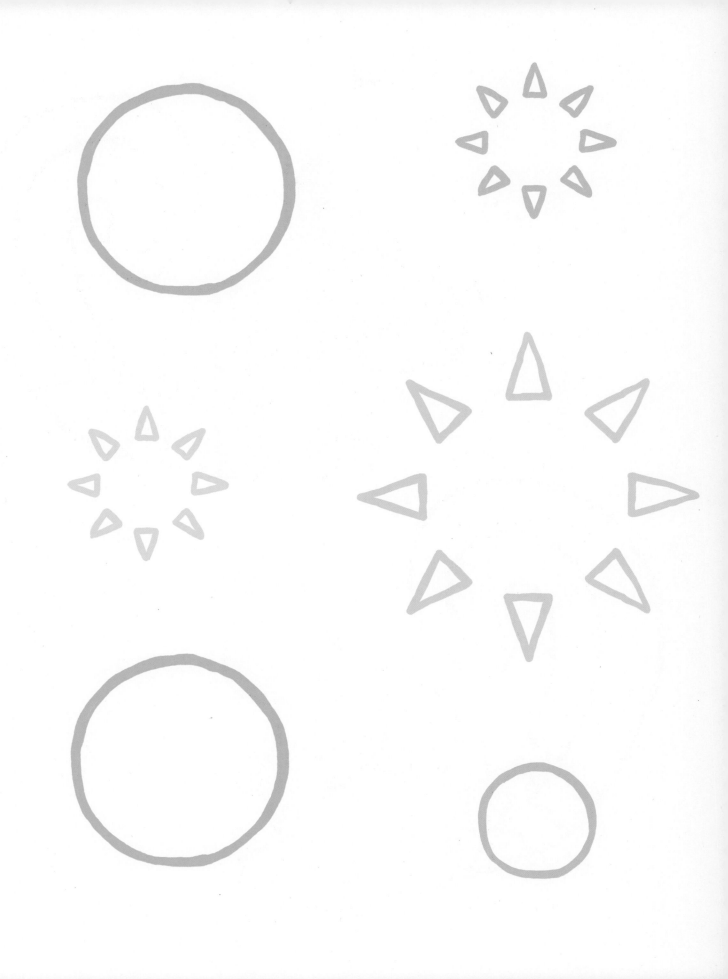

5 furry squirrels.

finish the pattern on each tail.

Raindrop patterns.
Add some more to make it pour!

Wavy patterns.
Add more wiggly lines.

Give every bird a pattern.

Count 5 little red birds.

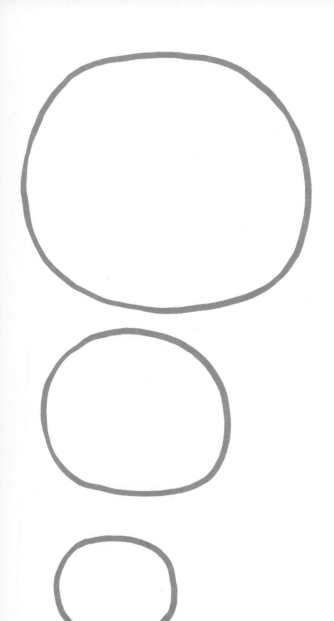

Someone's been shaking the bottles of soda.

Add more BIG and SMALL bubbles.

What a beautiful blanket, Bear!

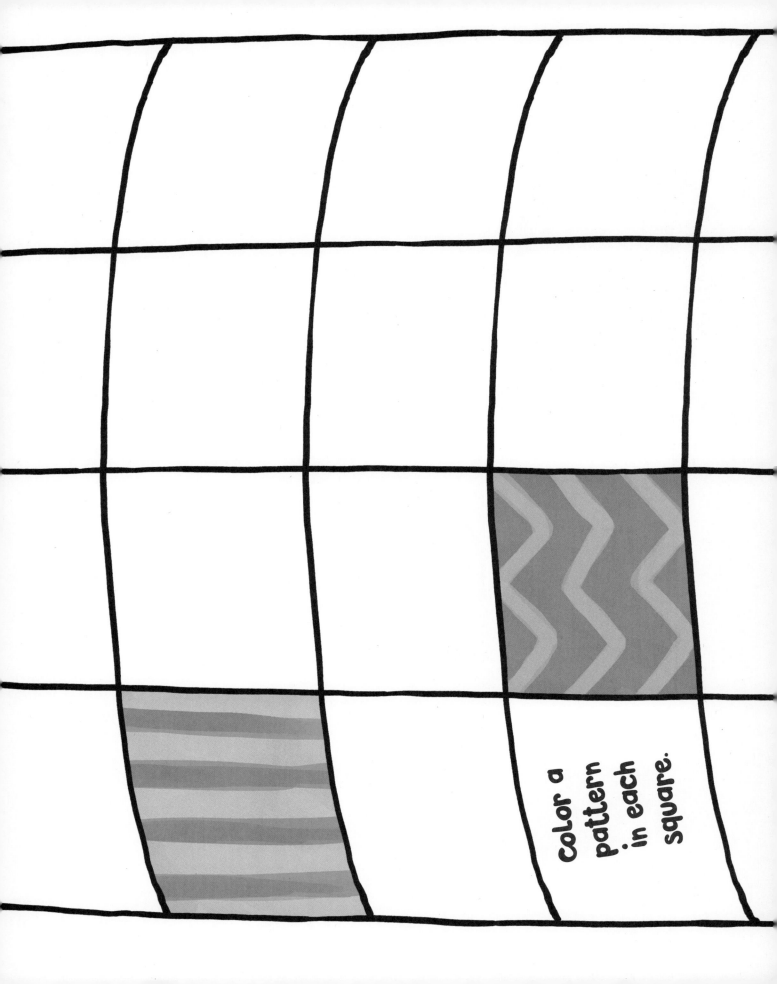

color a
pattern
in each
square.

Finish the patterns on each pretty dress.

Add triangles to each train to complete the patterns.

Try curls
and swirls.

Give Bear a big curly hairdo.

Pineapples!
special offer!

Fill the pineapples
with patterns.

who's watching the game?

Add faces and colorful patterns to the crowd.

Rabbit is redecorating.

Complete the
wallpaper patterns.

Fill in the missing shapes.

finish the pattern on each elephant.

finish coloring the pattern.

Wool Shop

Try some scribble balls.

Draw 3 pink balls.

Draw 4 green balls.

Add more red balls.

What is Rabbit knitting?

Draw something and fill it with a woolly pattern.

Draw straight Lines for Leaves.

Draw wiggly lines for bark.

color the pattern.

Give all the dogs spots!

Finish the squiggles.

Wheeee!

Add squiggles
to make
the cat
extra furry!

Puppies love puddles!

Add blobs to make
a puddly pattern!

Can-you-create-a-saurus?

Give them all
scaly patterns.

stomp, stomp, stomp!

What colorful patterns will you add to the hats?

Finish the check pattern by coloring the squares.

Color the squares on the shirts.

shaggy dogs! finish their hairy patterns.

Give him a wavy pattern.

Give him a zigzag pattern.

Turn this pattern into friendly fish!

Make a pattern with as many bubbles as you can!

Decorate the plain sails with patterns.

shh! The owls are sleeping.
finish their feather patterns.

finish coloring the pattern.

Fill the page with a big button pattern.

These porcupines
should all be
very spiky!

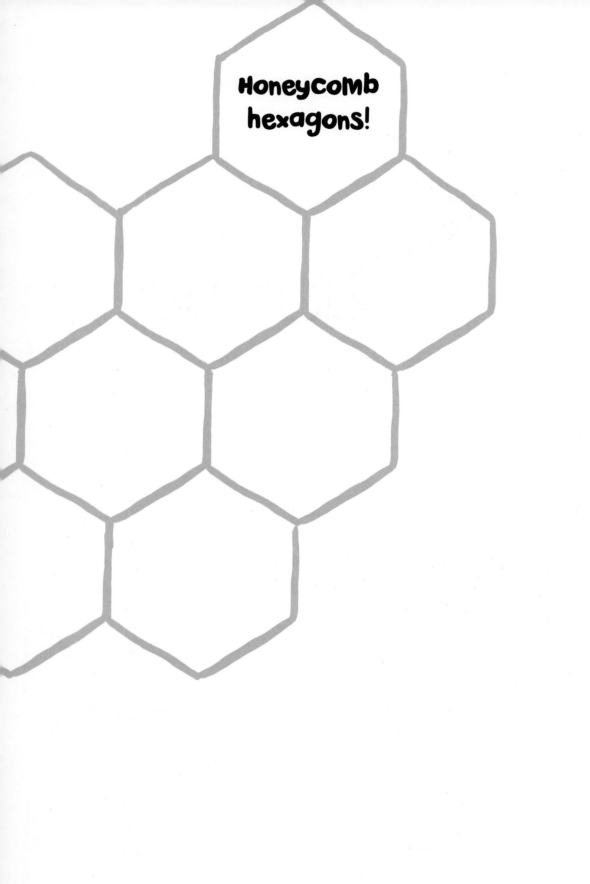

Honeycomb hexagons!

Make all the bees stripy.

circles make perfect flowers.

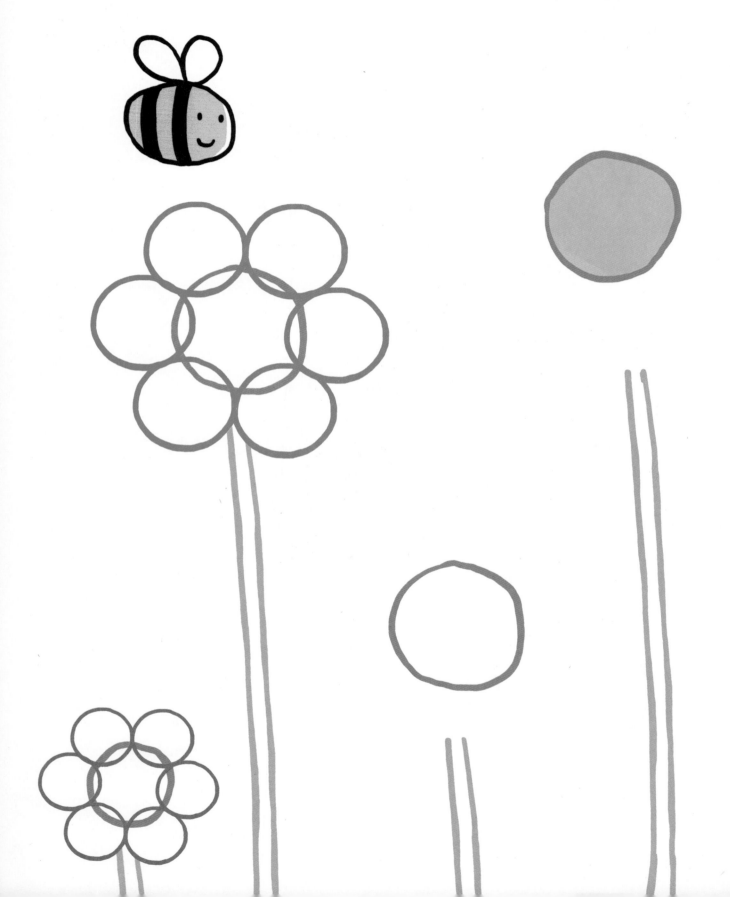

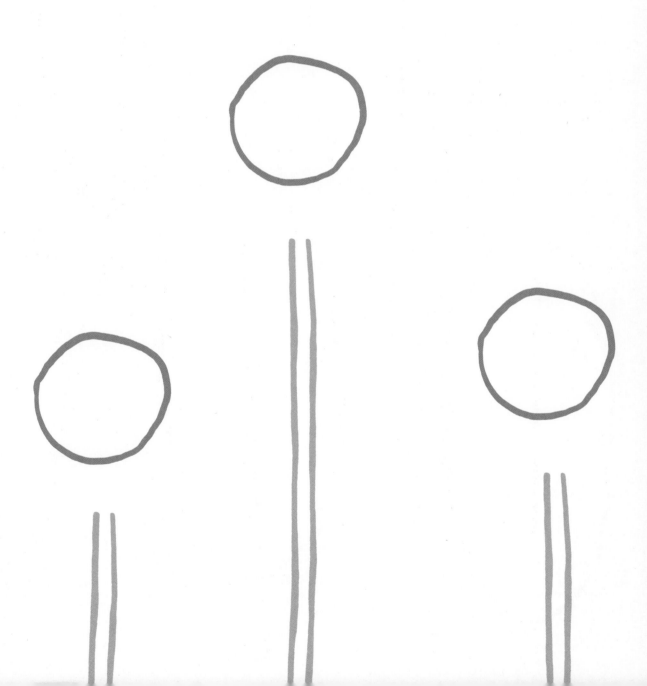

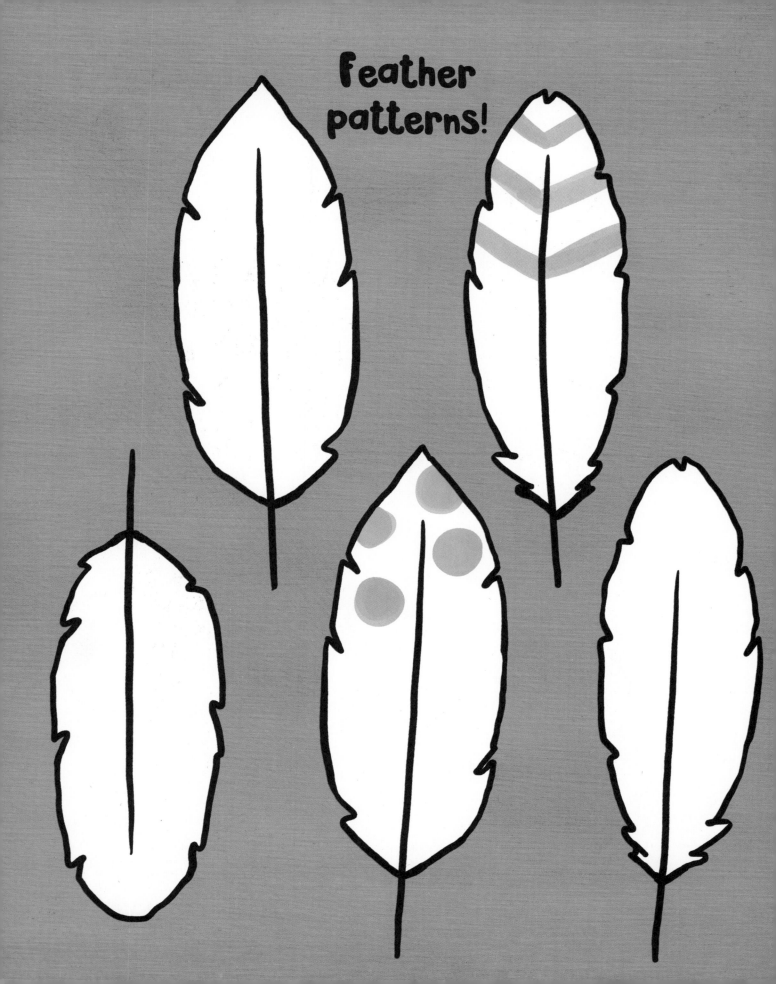

Feather patterns!

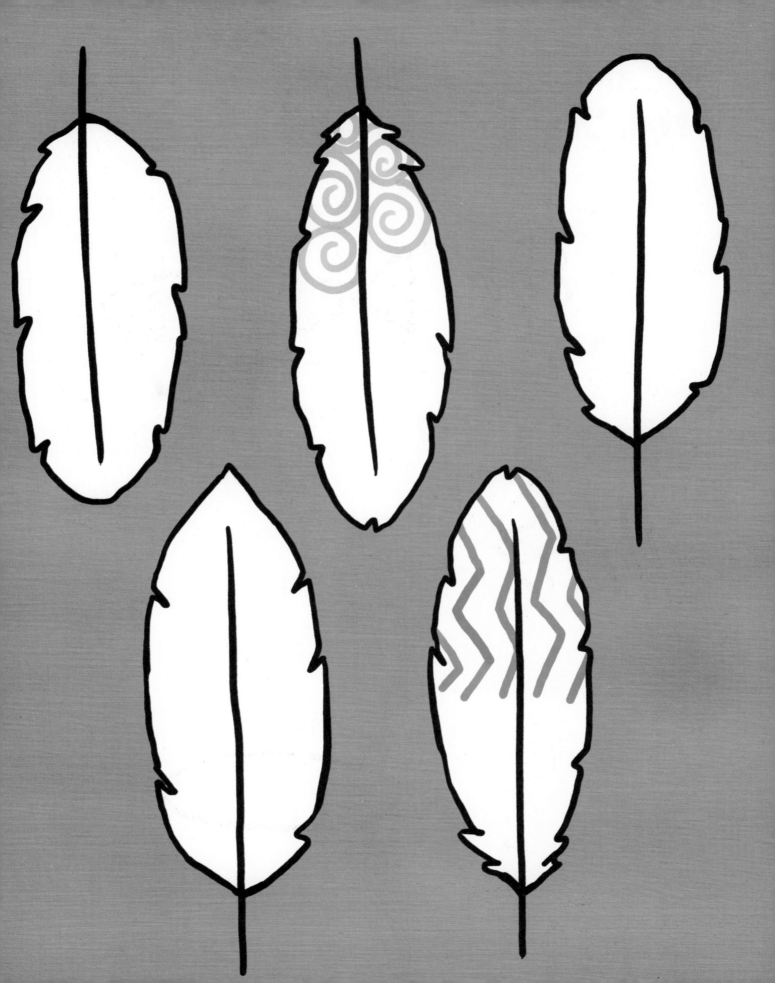

Put shapes and patterns together to make fish!

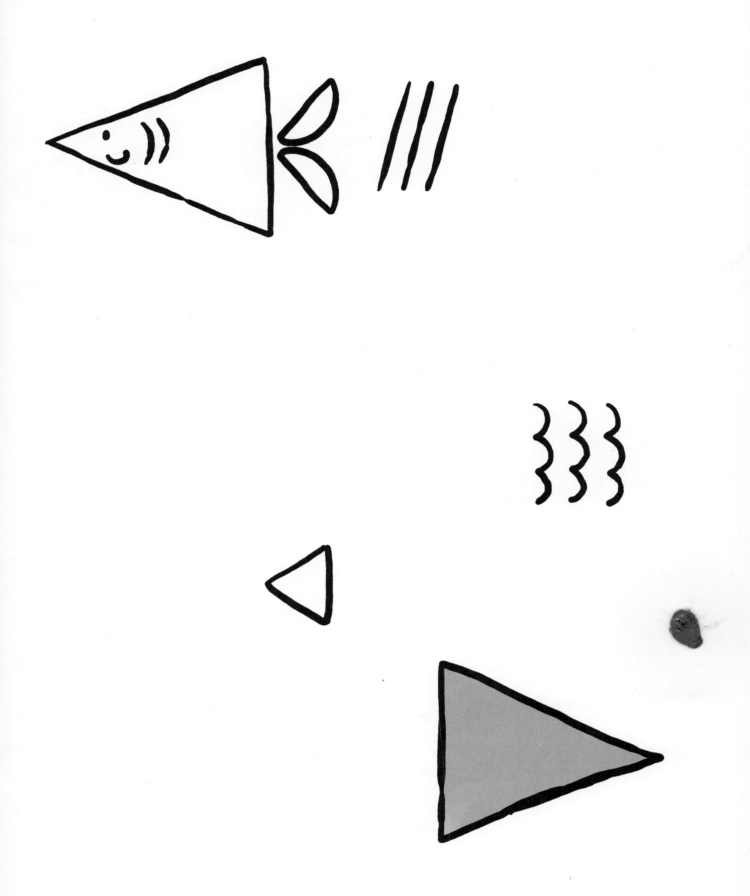

Add lines and zigzags to give every lion a magnificent mane.

Make a hand pattern.

Draw around your own hands to add more!

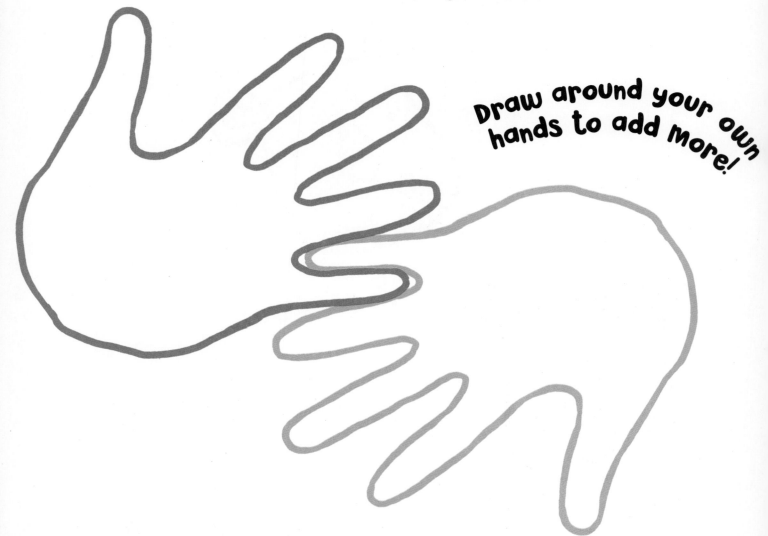

Add a pattern to each planet.

Finish the tire track patterns.

Turn this pattern into colorful penguins!

count 20 animals!

2

3

4

Give them all a pattern.

Delicious!

Decorate the donuts with patterns.

Add colorful patterns to all the scarves and hats.

1 tall giraffe

Finish his splotchy pattern!